TRANSFORM

31 DAYS
to Finding Your Identity in Christ
TONY MYLES

Copyright 2012 by Barefoot Ministries®

ISBN 978-0-8341-5116-1

Printed in the United States of America

Editor: Audra C. Marvin
Cover Design: J.R. Caines
Interior Design: Sharon Page

Library of Congress Cataloging-in-Publication Data: 2012939275

10 9 8 7 6 5 4 3 2 1

CONTENTS

INTRODUCTION

So . . . What do you want?

That's a seemingly innocent question that distracts many people on a daily basis. You likely think about it and probably have ever since an adult came up to you when you were a kid and asked, "What do you want to be when you grow up?"

It comes up all the time.

When a coach challenges, "Do you want to be first or second string?"

When friends wonder, "What do you want to do this weekend?"

When your parents question, "How do you want to spend the money in your pocket?"

Goals aren't always bad, but starting with this one each day can cause you to make harmful compromises to your true, God-given identity. What if what you want isn't good for you, but you think it is? Isn't this why some people change—to get the approval of others, such as someone they want to date or impress? Maybe you've seen this happen in a friend, perhaps even in yourself.

Our feelings can overtake our sense of judgment and start to rule every decision we make. Why else do you think grocery stores put candy in the checkout aisle?

We want to feel loved, so we run after it too fast or by the wrong rules and watch it turn to ashes once we wrap our arms around it. We want to feel appreciated, so we complain or manipulate situations to get others to applaud for us, even if it means wearing a fake mask that hides who we really are. We want to be in control of something, so we tell people to listen to us because we're leaders, instead of becoming people of integrity whom people actually want to follow.

We want to feel secure in life, so we surround ourselves with stuff that crumbles to pieces when we lean on it. We want to stop feeling the funk we feel we're in but refuse the discipline it takes to become who God says we can be.

It's why the Bible warns us in Jeremiah 17:9, "The heart is deceitful above all things and beyond cure. Who can understand it?" We all know what that verse is talking about because we've all been duped into thinking something that sounded good for a moment was actually good for us. You also see this when you sometimes do or say something in a moment that surprises you when you think about it later on.

Every story has a beginning, and you need to decide what yours will be. Either it starts with how you're feeling, or it starts with God and an identity that leads to freedom. Maybe you're tired of the way things are, and you've started to realize that flying by the seat of your pants in life isn't working anymore (and it never really did). It's time for a new identity—your real, God-given one, actually.

Jesus Christ offers you the most amazing fresh start, and it begins by seeing God for who he is in order to see yourself as he sees you. After all, he is your Creator and knows more about you than the rest of the world does. In light of all of this, he's even said you're worth dying for. That's just one glimpse of how awesome he is, which can help you realize how he sees you.

Something extraordinary happened when you were born. The world was given you—a gift that never before existed and never will again. God has a purpose for your life that is just as unique. Over time that purpose and the real you have been labeled something else, whether by people with great intentions or awful motives. Criticism like that can wear you down to the point that you forget who you even are anymore.

Check out God's insight on this, though, in 2 Corinthians 5:16-18: So from now on we regard no one from a worldly point of view. Though we once regarded Christ in this way, we do so no longer. Therefore, if anyone is in Christ, he is a new creation; the old has gone, the new has come! All this is from God, who reconciled us to himself through Christ and gave us the ministry of reconciliation. Every story has a beginning, but there is also a chapter when things turn around for the better, and your moment can happen now. But you need to stop asking for what you want. Instead, start finding out who God is and who he says you were born to be.

Can you imagine how different your life and the lives of others around you might be in a year if you stopped doing what merely made you happy in the moment and started doing what brought out the very best you? That's what that Corinthians verse ends on. This is more than a journey for you to go on by yourself; as God changes you from the inside out, you give hope to everyone around you by revealing him in the world. As you take off your mask and quit playing games with other people, you help others see Jesus in you so they might consider Jesus entering into them.

Welcome to that journey of changing the world from the inside out. Get ready to bump into your true identity along the way. Life as you know it is now over. At least, I hope so.

My name is Tony, and I've been on a journey with God that actively started when I was in high school. I was one of those guys who didn't know much about God, other than what I picked up through church services at Christmas and Easter. Even that was spotty. But my life has been filled with some of the most amazing joys, like my phenomenal wife, Katie, or my kids, Joshua, Daniel, and Johanna. I'm a part of an amazing church that does its best to keep the main thing the main thing. And after many years as a youth pastor, I really have a heart for the next generation.

On the other hand, my life has also been filled with some of the hardest wrestling matches I never would have imagined with God. Some of that happened through hard times when I wondered if I would make it, and other growth took place when I opened up the Bible and said, "God, what breaks your heart? Help it to break mine too."

So right now I hope you're willing to begin this journey with an ending; namely, that you're willing to become someone on the other side of this who more closely resembles who God made you to be. That may mean you leave big parts of your current way of thinking or doing behind, or maybe you're about to take part in several small adjustments that will blow you away.

We're going to journey through the book of James together because it's one of the most practical books on becoming a real-deal Christian. I hope you take notes—not just in this book but on your heart.

DAY 1

YOUR STARTING POINT

James 1:1
James, a servant of God and of the Lord Jesus Christ,
To the twelve tribes scattered among the nations: Greetings.

YOUR OBSERVATION

What are three ways James identifies himself?
(Hint: One is his name.)

A servant of God.
Scattered among the twelve tribes.

YOUR REACTION

What are three words you could use to identify you?

Funny
Outgoing
Short

YOUR DISCOVERY

Everybody is known by something to the rest of the world. Sometimes it's your name or perhaps the family you come from. Other times it's what you do or an experience that creates a certain nickname someone else gives you.

At the beginning of the book of James, the author identifies himself to his readers. It's commonly thought that this individual was actually a half-brother to Jesus,[1] born to Mary and Joseph after Jesus. Most people might use such credentials to their advantage and toss it around to gain some authority. Instead, he identifies himself as "James, a servant of God and of the Lord Jesus Christ."

What kind of humility do you imagine it takes for James to say that? After all, it's possible he grew up seeing things in Jesus that the rest of the world didn't. Perhaps some of those moments were extraordinary, but many were likely everyday things like eating, sleeping, laughing, singing, and doing chores around the house. Is it possible for all of that have made him miss out on seeing the core identity of Jesus until much later?

YOUR CHALLENGE

It's funny how you can have known somebody since you were little and yet not honestly know much about that person. Think about it. You may have classmates you've grown up with since kindergarten, but you don't know as much about them as you think you do.

Do you know how hard the kid sitting next to you in English really has it or what it's like for him to try to talk to his dad about his feelings? What about how hard it is for the girl in your neighborhood who looks in the mirror every day and sees a distortion of who she truly is? Are the athletes you know playing their sports because they like it or because they feel like they have to? Is the group of girls who dress in surprising ways really as carefree as they appear, or is it all a smokescreen?

Do you see people for who they really are, or do you see what they want you to see?

YOUR APPLICATION

Imagine you are given a superpower for one day to hear the thoughts of the people around you. This new ability may have its perks, but you'll also have to listen to the different things people struggle with inside their minds. You'll hear what motivates them to do the things they do or act the way they act.

What kind of new perspective do you think you'll walk away with?

Alot of people aren't who I think they are.

Now turn that around. What if people around you could hear your thoughts? What kind of perspective about you would they walk away with?

That Im a christian.

Obviously, this superpower doesn't exist, but Christians can walk around each day trying to listen to the Holy Spirit of God in order to respond to him. He has insights to offer on what's happening around you, but it will require you letting your day be more than what it commonly is.

What will you do differently tomorrow to let your identity be

_____Tessa_____, *a servant of God and of the Lord Jesus*
insert your name

Christ?

DAY 2

YOUR STARTING POINT

James 1:2-4

Consider it pure joy, my brothers, whenever you face trials of many kinds, because you know that the testing of your faith develops perseverance. Perseverance must finish its work so that you may be mature and complete, not lacking anything.

YOUR OBSERVATION

The challenge in this verse is to take joy in something that doesn't seem joyful. What role do you think God can play in helping you do this?

YOUR REACTION

If you were to apply this principle, what is one area of your life that might feel different than it does right now?

YOUR DISCOVERY

When James is inspired by God to share these powerful words, he likely doesn't know how he is going to die. The first-century historian Josephus writes that James was killed by stoning,[2] while the scholar Eusebius records that James was thrown from a building one hundred feet high then attacked and killed by a mob.[3] They agree that James was killed for his faith and endured a hard trial in his death.

James knows more than these large problems, though. He's called an apostle in Galatians 1:9, which means he is sent on a specific mission to lead a community of others into a growing faith in Jesus. Specifically, James is the leader of the church in Jerusalem, a region known for high religious tension. Imagine what he experiences on a daily basis simply by being right in the middle of the Roman government trying to rule the Jews while the Jewish leaders try to keep Christianity from spreading.

YOUR CHALLENGE

Chances are, you've had some tough experiences in your life; you've felt overwhelmed, scared, angry, or frustrated. Maybe you've felt let down by someone you care about or experienced an embarrassing moment when all eyes were on you. Sometimes these events leave a deep memory of pain that you feel like you'll never fully recover from, and it feels like you carry it around with you every day.

What the Bible reveals is that your pain will either *de*fine you or *re*fine you. You may not be able to change what happened in the past, what you're going through right now, or what you'll face tomorrow. But what you can control is how you will face it and whether you let your trials have the final word. Keep in mind, this isn't just the big stuff that you remember most but even the little annoyances in your day that can sour your overall attitude. Your identity does not have to be determined by the size of your problems; it can be determined by the size of your God.

▶ YOUR APPLICATION

Rank the following areas of your life in order of which problem areas seem to most affect your sense of who you are or what your attitude is like each day.
(Note: Some of these may not apply to you; mark them with an X.)

___ Parents not understanding me

___ Friends who say one thing yet do another

___ My transportation issues

___ The money challenges I have

___ My physical health

___ How out of control my life can feel

___ Cliques that don't include me

___ How my relationship with God feels at times

___ Confusion about my future

___ My grades

___ The way I'm treated in extracurricular activities

Pray, asking God to help you to focus less on these areas and more on him.

DAY 3

YOUR STARTING POINT

James 1:5-8

If any of you lacks wisdom, he should ask God, who gives generously to all without finding fault, and it will be given to him. But when he asks, he must believe and not doubt, because he who doubts is like a wave of the sea, blown and tossed by the wind. That man should not think he will receive anything from the Lord; he is a double-minded man, unstable in all he does.

YOUR OBSERVATION

James makes it clear that finding wisdom is something we need to ask God for, which implies that it doesn't always come naturally. What are other choices people might make when they don't know what to do instead of seeking the Lord?

(Example: Pretending they know what they're doing.)

YOUR REACTION

Where in your life do you lack wisdom, and what are you tempted to do instead of seek God for it?

YOUR DISCOVERY

The Greek word for wisdom that James uses is *sophia*, which means more than one type of wisdom. It can refer to everyday wisdom, such as things we learn by experience, find out by studying, or need to know in order to make good decisions. However, it can also mean the kind of wisdom that comes from God and counsels us in ways that are beyond human understanding.

Keep in mind that when you claim the promise of this scripture, it's not just asking God to give you all the answers without you doing any work. One way the Lord can answer your cry for wisdom is to put situations in your life where you can learn it, be it through other Christians or by reading something. He can also offer you an inner confidence and insight through his Holy Spirit, though, that will guide you forward in whatever area you are looking for his help.

YOUR CHALLENGE

The truth will set you free. But first, it will tick you off.

Let's face it. We'd rather live a don't-rock-the-boat life, where we call the shots. You can build a nice boat of a life, in fact, that is padded with comfortable seats and lots of the latest toys. You may even spend a lot of time filling it with things that make you feel good, as if you're the king of the world.

Then again, while that boat may seem expertly built and secure, it has a hole in it. Sometimes you'll see it, and sometimes you don't. Even weirder, sometimes you may see it and pretend you didn't.

So will you stay on this sinking Titanic, or will you accept the ladder of wisdom that just dropped from the rescue offered above? Out of all the courageous changes you must make in life, this shift is the hardest because it involves confessing that God knows more about your life than you do. That's more than just nodding your head or making an occasional appearance at a church service. It involves a life change that affects everything you are and everything you do.

That's why truth will tick you off.

The upside, though? Its momentum can tick you off the sinking boat, if you let it.

▶ YOUR APPLICATION

Do you understand what it means to have a saving relationship with Jesus Christ? God's wisdom is available to you but will only be clear if you really have begun a life-changing connection with him. If you haven't yet taken these steps, consider what they mean for you, step forward, and share your decision to follow through on this with a trusted adult you think can cheer you on.

Acknowledge God for who he is—your Creator who has a great plan for your life.

Believe that what he says is true—that you don't have to stay stuck in your sin.

Commit your life to Jesus Christ—through his sacrifice on the cross.

Decide that there is no turning back—whether life gets easier or harder.

Enjoy the journey—allow the Holy Spirit to lead your life each day.

DAY 4

YOUR STARTING POINT

James 1:9-11

The brother in humble circumstances ought to take pride in his high position. But the one who is rich should take pride in his low position, because he will pass away like a wild flower. For the sun rises with scorching heat and withers the plant; its blossom falls and its beauty is destroyed. In the same way, the rich man will fade away even while he goes about his business.

YOUR OBSERVATION

Notice how, in this passage, a rich person is considered to be in a low position, while a person who is struggling is said to be in a high position. Think about a practical example of this from what you've seen. For instance: Some may want to be popular but don't realize that they have to keep pleasing others to be popular. Yet someone who doesn't worry about this may feel less pressure from others.

YOUR REACTION

Is there a type of life that you crave and are frustrated that you don't have? If so, describe it here.

YOUR DISCOVERY

James is sometimes referred to as James the Just and was known for taking part in the Nazarite vow.[4] This was a process of giving up certain things—such as haircuts and anything that came from a vine tree—in order to prepare your life to better serve God. Personal sacrifices like this involve humility. James missed out on things that others took part in. The character and reputation that it formed, though, made him one of the great leaders of the early church.

 ## YOUR CHALLENGE

One of the toughest questions not to ask is, *What's in it for me?* We often want to know if we're going to get what we think we deserve, and we get crabby when we're overlooked or someone else gets more attention. Sometimes we even complain out loud about how our lives aren't like someone else's.

Humility isn't about making you or your life sound bad. It is about not stealing the spotlight or demanding to be in it. This will check your motives in situations really fast because a big part of discovering your true identity involves figuring out what drives you on the inside. It's easy to form and reflect a positive sense of self when you're doing well, but it's more genuine to see what comes out of you when life isn't going your way. A guy named Job experienced horrible hardships, and the Bible records him telling his wife, "Shall we [only] accept good from God, and not trouble?"[5]

 ## YOUR APPLICATION

What obstacles might prevent you from seeing the humble circumstances of your life as a blessing? Identify how your pride or sense of entitlement sometimes keeps you from praising God and becoming the kind of person he says you're capable of being.

DAY 5

YOUR STARTING POINT

James 1:12

Blessed is the man who perseveres under trial, because when he has stood the test, he will receive the crown of life that God has promised to those who love him.

YOUR OBSERVATION

James describes the reward of a "crown of life" given to those who persevere under trial. What are some examples you can think of in our culture that are like this for people who make it all the way to the end of something? (Example: the Super Bowl trophy)

YOUR REACTION

When have you wanted to give up on something but hung on and persevered because of the reward?

YOUR DISCOVERY

During the first century, the early Christians were often misunderstood, criticized, beat up, and mocked for their faith in Jesus. They weren't popular in many places, and even when something amazing happened, they often had to face something incredibly difficult. Simply put, there weren't a lot of rewards on the surface for the sacrifices they made.

Yet, in spite of it all, James and the other Christians in his day kept pressing on. As he says in this passage, there was a reward at the end of it all that he knew he would see. At times, that might mean something special on earth, while for other things it simply meant knowing there would be an eternal benefit when all was said and done. Somehow this was enough for them. The early Christians didn't find their identities in pats on the back but in being faithful to Jesus Christ.

 ## YOUR CHALLENGE

There's probably something in your life right now that you want to give up on. Maybe you should because it's tearing you away from the person God has made you to be. On other hand, this may be the very thing the Lord is using to chisel out your character and form something new in you.

You're probably going to have to pray on this, but there is one thing you can know for sure. If what you're doing is causing you or other people to sin, then you absolutely need to give it up. That may mean breaking up with someone you're dating who is dragging you down spiritually, emotionally, or physically. You're not going to do anyone any good by staying a part of that.

Where it gets tricky is if you're doing something productive for the Lord. While it's better to be an active Christian versus a lazy one, you have to make sure that the work you're doing for God isn't destroying the work of God in you. If it isn't, though, hang in there and keep pressing on until you have given 100% of your effort. Whether it's someone you're trying to share Jesus with who is resisting, or you're simply being faithful and showing integrity in a commitment you made, cross the finish line arm in arm with Jesus. There's nothing like knowing you took part in something beyond yourself that lasts forever.

YOUR APPLICATION

Make a list of the good things you're doing right now that have some measure of struggle to them. List the potential rewards you might gain by sticking with it.

Situation	Reward
Example: I will treat my family with love and respect, even when I want to be mean to them.	*God's pleasure; better relationship with my family; a more peaceful home life; won't get grounded.*
Example: I will stick with my part-time job, even though some days I can't stand it.	*I'll learn skills I can carry into a full-time job someday; I might get a raise; I can show Jesus to others in how I respond.*

DAY 6

YOUR STARTING POINT

James 1:13-15

When tempted, no one should say, "God is tempting me."
For God cannot be tempted by evil, nor does he tempt any-
one; but each one is tempted when, by his own evil desire, he is
dragged away and enticed. Then, after desire has conceived, it gives
birth to sin; and sin, when it is full-grown, gives birth to death.

YOUR OBSERVATION

James clarifies that God doesn't tempt us but instead wants us to be separated from sin. Why do you think this clarification has to be made? Do you know anyone who says, "It's okay that I do what I do. God made me this way. God gave me these desires."

YOUR REACTION

Notice how this verse says we can be "dragged away" by our own evil desires. Picture what that means. It's saying, "I don't want to go over there!" while running as hard as you can in that very direction. When have you done this?

YOUR DISCOVERY

While James lived in Jerusalem, he interacted with many people who knew the Hebrew Scriptures (what we call the Old Testament) inside and out. This might be part of the reason he specifically clarifies that sin doesn't come from God. The Jews regularly studied the first five books of the Bible, including Genesis, where the Bible records our earliest tendency to place the blame on others.

After Adam and Eve sin, Adam tells God, "The woman you put here with me—she gave me some fruit from the tree, and I ate it."⁶ Notice how Adam doesn't only point the finger at Eve but also sneaks in blaming the Lord. Since God created Eve for him, Adam tries to defend the ultimate bad (his own sin) by belittling the ultimate good (God himself).

 YOUR CHALLENGE

Most people tend to miscalculate the amount of temptation they can truly handle. Not only are we not good at anticipating the power of our urges; we also misjudge how much self-control we actually have. If we kept a more honest perspective about our willpower, we might better avoid putting ourselves in situations where our strongest temptations thrive and grow.

One way is to consider the B.L.A.H.S. in your life:
- Why do you end up doing what you do when you're Bored?
- How do you handle feeling Lonely?
- When do you first cross the line when you're feeling Angry?
- Where do you look for false affirmation when you're Hurting?
- What is different about your personality when you're Sleepy?

▼ **YOUR APPLICATION**

The dictionary tells us what the word *tempt* means:
- To entice or allure to do something often regarded as unwise, wrong, or immoral.
- To attract, appeal strongly to, or invite.
- To render strongly disposed to do something.
- To put to the test in a venturesome way; provoke: to tempt one's fate.

Rewrite each of those definitions below, using a situation from your own life.

Example: I was enticed to make out with someone at a party in ways that are unwise, wrong, or immoral.

Your version:

Example: I was attracted in a strong way to someone at my school who tempts me away from God.

Your version:

Example: After watching that TV show, I was more strongly disposed to think of sex before marriage as less of a big deal.

Your version:

Example: I was really put to the test when I wanted to hit my brother in anger.

Your version:

ID CHECK

Read: John 1:12

What have you learned in the past six days about who God says you can become?

In what areas might you be falling short the most in claiming your God-given identity?

What is one action step you can put into place over the next seven days to grow more fully into your identity in Christ?

DAY 8

⬦ YOUR STARTING POINT

James 1:16-18

*Don't be deceived, my dear brothers. Every good and
perfect gift is from above, coming down from the Father of
the heavenly lights, who does not change like shifting shadows. He
chose to give us birth through the word of truth, that we might be a
kind of firstfruits of all he created.*

◀ YOUR OBSERVATION

What are some of the gifts God has given you to enjoy by being a Christian? (If you need some ideas, read Galatians 5:22-23.)

▌ YOUR REACTION

We all have friends who seem to change on us, at times. What comfort
do you take in knowing that God doesn't change?

How might you be tempted to take advantage (in a selfish way) of the
fact that God doesn't change?

YOUR DISCOVERY

The concept of firstfruits refers to sacrifices people made to God from their harvests. While he didn't need any of this, it was a practice where people gave their very best to him—a certain amount from the first parts of their new crops—to remember who he was (their ultimate provider) and who they were (grateful receivers). Christians recognize this today by giving at least 10% of their income to God as a tithe that supports the work of his church.

In this verse, though, the concept kicks up a notch. It's not talking about what we give God but how he has given us to the world. This means the Lord sees you as one of his very best ideas and gifts to those who haven't yet come to know him personally. Soak that in because it's one of the highest compliments God could give you!

YOUR CHALLENGE

Your family and friends may be some of the most imperfect people you know. It's not that anyone else is more perfect than them, but you are more familiar with the faults of those closest to you because you spend the most time with them. You see who they are when no one else is looking, and it can cause you to become critical of them.

Maybe you're allowing their imperfections to make them seem more flawed than they really are. Even an imperfect gift can be realized as a perfect gift from God if that person helps you grow closer to him. In fact, the gift of that person might be absolutely perfect, but the packaging may be what's messed up.

Pray, and ask God to help you praise him more often for what he's given you. Develop an attitude of gratitude that not only becomes contagious in your relationships but allows you the chance to see your own potential to grow—imperfections and all.

◣ YOUR APPLICATION

Spend a few moments writing down how some of God's perfect gifts can help you form an identity that sees other imperfect things differently.

Because God gives me the fect gift of . . .	**I can view this imperfect per-thing/person in this way:**
Love	
Joy	
Peace	
Patience	
Kindness	
Goodness	
Faithfulness	
Gentleness	
Self-Control	

DAY 9

◢ YOUR STARTING POINT

James 1:19-20
My dear brothers, take note of this: Everyone should be quick to listen, slow to speak and slow to become angry, for man's anger does not bring about the righteous life that God desires.

◀ YOUR OBSERVATION

Consider what *isn't* in this passage. We're not told that anger is wrong but that there is a right way to become angry. Why do you think this is, and what do you think is the difference between slow anger and fast anger?

▌ YOUR REACTION

Think of the last three times you became really angry over something. Which would you describe as slow anger, and which can you identify as fast anger?

◣ YOUR DISCOVERY

There's a reason we're spending time in the book of James. We've already identified James as a brother to Jesus, but what you may not know is there was a time that he and his siblings didn't believe in the miraculous power of Christ. In John 7:5, Matthew 12:47, and Mark 3:31, we read about how, at one point, they simply didn't give the Lord any credibility.

Imagine how foolish James felt later on when he saw the risen Jesus after Peter, the twelve, and the five hundred had seen him (1 Corinthians 15:7). Before that, James probably saw Jesus as an annoying brother who said foolish things. If only he had been quick to listen, slow to speak, and slow to become angry.

 YOUR CHALLENGE

The things people say or do can radically change our world in an instant. Maybe your favorite website changes its format, or your phone breaks, and you have to adapt to a new one. Someone in your family can say something that affects everyone else, or a friend breaks the news that he's moving away. It may just be that an authority figure over you tells you that you're not going to get your way.

Have you ever paid attention to how you handle yourself in such moments? Maybe you're quick to get frustrated, say something passionate, or blast your anger at the world. Some people become activists and organize every person they can think of to protest what's happened, talking about the way things are supposed to be. Others become demolitionists, deciding that they will talk *about* people and tear them down instead of talk *with* people and build a bridge. There are those who become invisible, avoiding addressing the frustration or person at all costs. Also, some become diggers who take the stuff that frustrates them and bury it somewhere out of sight (but still there).

Take note of the directions we're given in this passage, though, to be quick to listen, slow to speak, and slow to become angry. Imagine how different certain situations in your life could have been if you or another person had followed this command. We spend so much time cleaning up what we've wasted instead of building priorities that give life.

YOUR APPLICATION

Consider the three steps and what this means logistically for you in becoming a person who regularly practices this approach:

The Command	What I must do more of	What I must do less of
Be quick to listen.		
Be slow to speak.		
Be slow to become angry.		

DAY 10

YOUR STARTING POINT

James 1:21
*Therefore, get rid of all moral filth and the evil that is so prevalent
and humbly accept the word planted in you, which can save you.*

YOUR OBSERVATION

According to this passage, the word *evil* refers to something that is
prevalent or frequently seen in the world. If God were to look at this
culture today, what might he specifically say is evil?

YOUR REACTION

If people were to point out things in your life that you either take part in
or tolerate as evil, what might your first reaction to them be?

YOUR DISCOVERY

You know when this was written? The first century. Now here you are,
twenty centuries later, reading something that applies to your life. James
may not have portable electronic devices where he can access filthy con-
tent online or cell phones that allow him to send profane texts and media

to his friends, but still the command remains to get rid of all the moral filth and evil that is all over the place.

God's truths are not written in a history book. They are written in his Bible. This is an eternal compilation of the stuff that matters most in the whole world, and that's why, even though James may be talking about something specific in his day, it applies to our day too. The word we translate as *filth* was originally *rupos*, which can mean "dirt that soils clothes" or "ear wax." It's as if he's saying, "Whatever it is that is causing you to stink because it's on you, or is blocking your ability to hear God because it's clogging up your ears, get rid of it!"

 YOUR CHALLENGE

Temptations are just a part of life, and we will constantly face them until we're finally in heaven. Each time we're tempted, the key is not to ask, *What do I want to do here?* but, *Who am I, and who will I be in this moment?* You can't change your behavior permanently until you permanently change your identity, and only God can make that possible. If you let him, that is.

Even if you've established this, though, there is still some work to do. Recognize not only the areas of your life where you are most tempted but also *when* you are tempted—such as the time of day, or if you're by yourself or with others. You may need to establish some accountability with a friend or family member to help you avoid situations where you find yourself embracing your old identity created by sin, instead of your new identity created by God.

There's one other thing that you may initially not want to hear. You might need to give up some of your favorite movies, TV shows, books, magazines, music, or websites that encourage you to enjoy or not mind things that break God's heart. If you struggle with lust, it might be time to tear down that poster of your favorite hottie or erase some of the half-naked (or fully naked) pictures you have saved on your computer. It could be that your fiction is getting in the way of truth, and you're going to have to ask yourself which matters most.

 **YOUR APPLICATION**

What is the dirt that stains or ear wax in your life that you need to get rid of?

Things I own or have access to that distract me from hearing or following God:

People I know who distract me from hearing or following God:

YOUR STARTING POINT

James 1:22-25

Do not merely listen to the word, and so deceive yourselves. Do what it says. Anyone who listens to the word but does not do what it says is like a man who looks at his face in a mirror and, after looking at himself, goes away and immediately forgets what he looks like. But the man who looks intently into the perfect law that gives freedom, and continues to do this, not forgetting what he has heard, but doing it—he will be blessed in what he does.

YOUR OBSERVATION

The metaphor of a mirror is used to describe paying attention for a moment but not living out what you saw. What is another metaphor or comparison you could make like this? (Example: It's like ordering at a restaurant and not eating any of the food.)

YOUR REACTION

Underline the words in the scripture above that most represent what you tend to do. Circle the parts that represent action steps for you to take or things you want to experience from God.

YOUR DISCOVERY

Ancient mirrors weren't made of glass. They were made of highly polished metal. This implied that they weren't used to admire your face (because it would seem quite dim and marked up) but that you looked into a mirror to *do* something. James is talking here about the same idea—that a Christian is to look into God's Word to learn who he or she is, and do something about it.

This tracks back to how, in the ancient world, it was common for people to sit around and hear a teacher teach in a public area. Anybody could listen in, but many would get up and leave to go do whatever they did before. If you followed that teacher, though, and tried to live out what he said, then you were called a disciple of that teacher.

YOUR CHALLENGE

Think about what would happen if you walked into your neighbors' home and acted like you lived there. Maybe you'd walk in the front door, and they'd awkwardly greet you, and then you'd make your way over to the kitchen and grab a snack from the refrigerator. Your neighbors would likely start to raise their voices, but you'd ignore them and sit on the couch to watch TV. For a moment, there might be some confusion. Ultimately, though, they'd start trying to force you out of the house.

This is more than the plot of some weird movie. It's a false reality we try to create every day. It's like we wake up each day and look in the mirror but then head off and pretend we're somebody else. Not in terms of where we physically live or by changing our names but by making decisions that seem to reflect we don't live in God's family at all and instead live somewhere else.

Not only are the people around us confused, but it could be confusing to God (if he didn't know everything, that is). That doesn't make it any less important to him, though. All throughout the Bible, we read about how God is frustrated with the games his people play with him, saying they love him one moment and then building a false idol to worship the next moment.

So consider this question: Do you know where you live, and do you actually live there, or do you pretend like you live somewhere else?

YOUR APPLICATION

It takes more energy to be fake than it does to be real. Write down the different ways you've tried to appear to be someone you're not over the past week or so. Be honest, and think through even little lies you said to keep a conversation going, make a story sound more interesting, or appear exciting to others.

DAY 12

YOUR STARTING POINT

James 1:26-27

If anyone considers himself religious and yet does not keep a tight rein on his tongue, he deceives himself and his religion is worthless. Religion that God our Father accepts as pure and fault-less is this: to look after orphans and widows in their distress and to keep oneself from being polluted by the world.

YOUR OBSERVATION

Out of all the things God could affirm, why do you think he picks caring for widows and orphans?

YOUR REACTION

Can you think of times that you were being "religious," versus genuinely spending time with God or serving him out of an authentic love for him?

YOUR DISCOVERY

The word *religious*, or *religion*, means different things to different people, but in the Bible neither is used in a positive way. These words always hint at something people doing to try and feel spiritual but somehow fall short. Even today many Christians talk about how they have a relationship with God versus a mere religion.

James taps into this as well, describing people who believe they're right with Jesus Christ but keep saying things that hint at something else. Sometimes this reveals that people really aren't in a relationship with God at all, while other times it points to old habits that Christians haven't let God have control over. It's easy to overlook the fact that something as simple as the way you talk about others or the jokes you pass along can water down (and even eliminate) the authenticity of your faith.

On the other hand, doing something tangible, like caring for widows and orphans, gives credibility to your faith. Keep in mind, these actions aren't a substitute for a relationship with Jesus because even an atheist can do these things—hold their tongues or help others. James is talking about the power of being consistent and removing the obstacles from others seeing Jesus.

 YOUR CHALLENGE

Admit it: You like giving others a hard time (even though you know you shouldn't). You might even do it without realizing how others receive it. For example:

Maybe you enjoy giving little kids a hard time. (Little kid: "I'm hungry." You: "Hi, Hungry! Glad to meet you." Little kid: "STOPPPPPPPP!")

Perhaps you bring up old conversations whenever you see people ("Hey! It's Scary Toes! Hey everyone, this one time Sheila was wearing flip flops, and her toes were all dirty. Scary!")

Quite possibly you take shortcuts with names that other people haven't asked you to (Person: "Hi, I'm Nicholas." You: "Hey, Nick!")

It could be that you're the "Yeah, but . . ." person in every conversation, email, or online post. (Person: ". . . which is why I feel as strongly about that as I do." You: "Yeah, but how about this . . . ?")

Most of this has less to do with a conscious effort to anger others and more our own way of blowing off steam or processing life. Still, even though we'd claim, "That's just who I am," that doesn't mean it's who you should be. Sometimes our attempt not to feel annoyed by life actually ends up annoying others and blocks their sense of God in our lives. Or, as Proverbs 27:3 puts it, "Stone is heavy and sand a burden, but provocation by a fool is heavier than both."

YOUR APPLICATION

Rate your speech from 1 to 5, with 1 meaning rarely and 5 meaning often. Note the verse listed next to each, and commit to memorizing it for the ones you score the highest.

___ When I am angry with someone, I tell that person off. (Proverbs 15:1)

___ I help my friends get back at others through gossip. (Proverbs 17:9)

___ I unnecessarily talk about others when they aren't around. (Proverbs 11:13)

___ I share my opinion about others, no matter what it is. (Proverbs 10:19)

___ I speak before I stop to think about what I'm saying. (Proverbs 13:3)

___ I say things that hurt others. (Ephesians 4:29)

___ I listen to or tell dirty jokes. (Ephesians 4:29)

DAY **13**

James 2:1-4

My brothers, as believers in our glorious Lord Jesus Christ, don't show favoritism. Suppose a man comes into your meeting wearing a gold ring and fine clothes, and a poor man in shabby clothes also comes in. If you show special attention to the man wearing fine clothes and say, "Here's a good seat for you," but say to the poor man, "You stand there" or "Sit on the floor by my feet," have you not discriminated among yourselves and become judges with evil thoughts?

YOUR OBSERVATION

Do poor or rich people come to your church? How about popular people versus not so popular people? Why do you think it's easy for us to treat people differently based on their financial or social status?

YOUR REACTION

Who are the last five people you reached out to outside your comfort zone to have even a short, positive conversation?

◤ YOUR DISCOVERY

The people James writes to are used to being divided into categories. That doesn't mean they like it, but it is common—much like the people at school or in your life may do this. In James, sometimes people are categorized by the money they have or a job they hold, but most of the time it is about a person's religious or ethnic background. Even in religious gatherings, people are treated uniquely one way or another.

What is confusing is that God's people are called to be separate, and many Jews believe that this means they are the ones who will go on to be with the Lord into eternity while everyone else misses out. Jesus corrects this in John 4:22, saying, "Salvation is from the Jews." James takes it to the next level, making sure to knock down any of the walls we put between someone getting to connect with God.

YOUR CHALLENGE

It's been said that what you attract people with is what you'll need to use to keep them interested. In other words, you'll have to constantly outdo yourself over and over again with a slightly more twisted version of whatever you offered them in the beginning. It's kind of like a treadmill you can't keep up with, no matter how hard you run.

Sometimes you see this in how a movie sequel or the second season of a television series is a bit darker than the first. The creators know you liked what they did last time, so they throw in something new that will get your attention and keep it longer than before. Pop stars do this as well, sometimes doing controversial things over and over again to stay in the spotlight. Maybe you can even think of a few celebrities who started out normal but have gone downhill.

God doesn't want you to play that game, whether it's with your own identity or someone else's. Perhaps you've seen how showing one person favoritism requires you to do it again next time, or else that person will be let down. Likewise, it can hurt others to think that they don't matter as much as someone else, causing them to become someone they're not just to get noticed.

Think about all the energy you spend trying to keep people impressed and interested in your life. How much of it is surface level because you want popular people to like you? We may even think we're doing a good thing by showing favoritism in church or youth group because we think a popular person can lead more people to Jesus. Then again, Jesus didn't call the first string to be his disciples. . . . He called the guys who were hanging out in the parking lot because they couldn't afford a ticket to the game.

 YOUR APPLICATION

Fill in the blanks:

I'd like people to say I am the greatest _____

that they know.

The person I seem to give most of my attention to is

_____.

The person I give the least amount of my attention to is

_____.

DAY 14

ID CHECK

Read: Romans 8:1-2

What have you learned in the past six days about who God says you can become?

In what areas might you be falling short the most in claiming your God-given identity?

What is one action step you can put into place over the next seven days to grow more fully into your identity in Christ?

DAY 15

YOUR STARTING POINT

James 2:5-9

Listen, my dear brothers: Has not God chosen those who are poor in the eyes of the world to be rich in faith and to inherit the kingdom he promised those who love him? But you have insulted the poor. Is it not the rich who are exploiting you? Are they not the ones who are dragging you into court? Are they not the ones who are slandering the noble name of him to whom you belong? If you really keep the royal law found in Scripture, "Love your neighbor as yourself," you are doing right. But if you show favoritism, you sin and are convicted by the law as lawbreakers.

YOUR OBSERVATION

What kind of bullying do you see going on in this passage?

YOUR REACTION

What kind of bullying do you see going on in your life?

YOUR DISCOVERY

Back in the first century, money lending was popular between rich people and poor people. Most of the time it wasn't out of charity, though, for the rich planned to put the poor into a form of slavery. At any time, a rich person could grab someone off the street who owed him money, take him to court, and make the arrangements to legally have that man or woman work for him.

It's no wonder people feared the rich, even in church gatherings. To make someone with money feel happy, the poor gave up their seats or were asked by others to do so. This was all like an ancient version of a bully coming up to a weaker kid and demanding he turn over his seat and food during lunch.

There were rich people who weren't mean and abusive like this, and James isn't talking about them. It's absolutely fine to have a friendship with someone who has more money than you do and allow that person the same courtesy you would offer anyone else. What these verses warn against, though, is giving others special treatment because of their money or making the poor feel as if they don't matter in God's kingdom.

 YOUR CHALLENGE

It's easy to spot bullies who use their physical strength or presence to intimidate others. You might also be able to spot snobs who use their financial status to get others to do what they want. What may not be as easy to spot is the way that *you* are a bully or snob—because you likely are in some small way.

Before you defend yourself, think about the type of people you enjoy laughing about with your friends. Maybe it's justifiable, like someone who gets on everyone's nerves and is fun to talk about. Or perhaps it's a personality difference, like someone who is dull, has poor hygiene habits, or is into different things than you. We may not be hurting those people with our fists or words, but we definitely don't seek them out to become a part of our social circles.

You still may not think you're a bully, and maybe you're right. On the other hand, maybe you'd agree that there are some people you show special treatment to that others don't get. That may not feel like bullying, but not standing up for these people or inviting them in can set up someone else to be cruel to them.

▶ YOUR APPLICATION

Jesus offers you an identity that is to be like his. Since our Savior died for everyone, he challenges you to let your reputation die so everyone might be included. You likely know many people who don't know him and are in real danger of spending an eternity separated from God in a place described as unbearable and unending. So be honest and complete the circle below by writing down some names or categories of people. Then write the word **JESUS** in large letters over all of it when you're done.

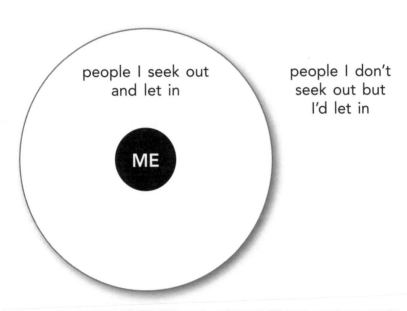

people I seek out
and let in

ME

people I don't
seek out but
I'd let in

people I don't seek out,
and don't really want to let in

DAY 16

YOUR STARTING POINT

James 2:10-13

For whoever keeps the whole law and yet stumbles at just one point is guilty of breaking all of it. For he who said, "Do not commit adultery," also said, "Do not murder." If you do not commit adultery but do commit murder, you have become a lawbreaker. Speak and act as those who are going to be judged by the law that gives freedom, because judgment without mercy will be shown to anyone who has not been merciful. Mercy triumphs over judgment!

YOUR OBSERVATION

Why do you think these verses had to be written? What do you imagine people were saying or doing before this?

YOUR REACTION

What sin in your life do you try to minimize because you think it's not as big of a deal as other things? You might have to think hard on this because you may have convinced yourself it's not even a sin. (Example: illegal music downloading)

YOUR DISCOVERY

The Jewish rabbis (religious leaders) held to the idea that if a person didn't believe even the smallest part of God's law, it was like saying none of it mattered.[7] God reveals the larger picture of this through this passage, showing that the same is true of our sin. While our rebellious attitude or actions don't need to be permanent if we turn to Jesus, they do create gaps in our relationship with the Lord. Even one gap can make a difference. Imagine a rope bridge across a huge chasm that is suddenly missing just a small, one-inch section. That one tiny disconnection will cause the whole bridge to fall apart.

YOUR CHALLENGE

Over the years, buffet restaurants have gained popularity. For a single price, you can pick and choose whatever you want and leave behind the less than desirable food. Many come with dessert bars and drink stations that give even more opportunities to make sure your dining experience is exactly how you want it to be.

You may want to do this to your relationship with God too. A lot of people don't want the Lord to overhaul their entire identities but only parts of them. Every little thing we hold back, though, becomes a much larger thing over time.

Every sin is different, but every sin counts as sin. To become a traffic lawbreaker, you don't have to speed at 120 miles an hour in a 40-mile-per-hour zone. You simply have to run a stop sign. This is what God is talking about when James writes how even one act of rebellion matters and separates us from God in its own way.

YOUR APPLICATION

Circle the top four things that you feel you struggle with and actually do the most.

Lie	Hurt others physically
Gossip	Put boyfriend/girlfriend before God
Lust on purpose	Covet/want what others have
Steal money	Dishonor your parents
Download music illegally	Cheapen God's name
Overeat	Don't share your faith

Pray, and ask God to help you get out of the rut of doing these things over and over.

DAY 17

YOUR STARTING POINT

James 2:14-18

What good is it, my brothers, if a man claims to have faith but has no deeds? Can such faith save him? Suppose a brother or sister is without clothes and daily food. If one of you says to him, "Go, I wish you well; keep warm and well fed," but does nothing about his physical needs, what good is it? In the same way, faith by itself, if it is not accompanied by action, is dead. But someone will say, "You have faith; I have deeds." Show me your faith without deeds, and I will show you my faith by what I do.

YOUR OBSERVATION

What do you think is more important: showing the world that you're a Christian or knowing you're a Christian?

YOUR REACTION

Which do you tend to do more of: live out your faith so others can see or quietly acknowledge your faith before God on the inside?

YOUR DISCOVERY

Critics of the early Christians struggled with the idea that all a person needed to do was agree with a few ideas about Jesus in order to be saved. This passage shows there is more to it than that, for faith isn't the ending but the beginning of giving your whole life to God. People of faith shouldn't have to be explained to the world because of inconsistencies but people whose lives can reveal the Lord if they live with integrity.

 ## YOUR CHALLENGE

It's one thing to say you believe in Jesus but another thing to let your everyday life reflect that. The songwriter Rich Mullins wrote that faith without works is "about as useless as a screen door on a submarine." You may have been raised in a Christian home or come to a moment where you wanted what Jesus offered, but you can't get to heaven on a prayer. Jesus didn't say, "Pray this, and you're in." He said, "Follow me," which means you need to decide if you're going to be a Christ follower or a church person who says a lot of things about Jesus.

A lot of teenagers who call themselves Christians swing back and forth between different identities, all based on who they're around and what they're doing. When others aren't looking, many take part in activities and behaviors that don't honor Christ. Others, though, understand that being a Christian is an identity that determines everything else. It's one thing to know a lot of things about God and another thing for God to say, "I know that kid, and that kid knows me."

You may have had a great start to your faith by receiving the gift of Jesus Christ, but not living out the fullness of that gift with your actions makes about as much sense as hitting a home run and standing at home plate instead of running the bases. Don't let your life become a dressed-up version of your old one, where you say more spiritual things and take part in more church stuff. You may not ever be perfect in this, but you do need to make a decision which identity you will live in: one that seeks to know and serve Jesus better or one that is intentionally inconsistent on a regular basis.

 **YOUR APPLICATION**

Jesus said to love the Lord with all of our hearts, souls, minds, and strength. He also said to love our neighbors as we love ourselves. Practically speaking:

Because I love God with my heart, I will let my heart break over . . .

Because I love God with my soul, I will put this first in my life:

Because I love God with my mind, I will fill my thought life up with . . .

Because I love God with my strength, I will let everything I have be used for . . .

Because I love God with my relationships, I will be the kind of friend who . . .

DAY 18

YOUR STARTING POINT

James 2:19
You believe that there is one God. Good! Even the demons believe that—and shudder.

YOUR OBSERVATION

This is one of a handful of verses in the Bible that describes demons. What can you learn about them from this one verse all by itself?

YOUR REACTION

Read Mark 12:29-31, and then write down your understanding of what it means that there is "one God," or that "God is one."

YOUR DISCOVERY

James cites the difference between believing in God and having a life that lives out a faith in him. Demons are mentioned because they essentially have a factual faith in God and acknowledge that he exists but don't celebrate it. After all, demons know that one day they will face the torment of being judged by the Almighty for their actions.

You can compare this to a teacher, coach, or principal whom some people don't like but have to respect because of that person's authority. Some of the Christians James writes to have the same problem in that they want all the benefits God offers without actually following him with their lives. At times people do this on purpose, while others believe that all they need to do is say that God runs the world and is Lord over everything. What both overlook is having a life that actually lives for him.

YOUR CHALLENGE

There's a big difference between believing in something and putting your entire faith into it. People can believe that a parachute can save them if they jump out of an airplane, but that's a big difference from actually strapping on a parachute, leaping out the plane door, falling at incredible speeds, and pulling the ripcord. Those people have proved that they have knowledge as well as faith to follow through.

Imagine that you are suddenly put on trial for being a Christian. Someone will investigate your life by talking to people you know, looking through your stuff, checking into the movies or TV shows you've watched, reading your internet history, tracking how you spend your time and money, and asking you questions about what you've done with your life. Will there be enough evidence to convict you for being a Christian, or will they have a hard time finding any proof?

YOUR APPLICATION

Don't skip over the mention of demons in this passage. You may know that you have a personal Savior in Jesus, but you may not realize that you have a personal enemy in Satan. The devil is not only against you; he is also after your friends and family.

Prayer offers an incredibly powerful connection with God that helps you become more aware of what is happening on this level. Sometimes spiritual warfare is like the wind. You can't see it with your eyes, but you see the effects of it in the world. Read Ephesians 6:10-20 then pray for protection over your friends and family by name. Ask God to help them do more than merely acknowledge that he exists but fully trust their lives into his hands. Then watch for any opportunities God offers you to share his message.

DAY 19

YOUR STARTING POINT

James 2:20-26

You foolish man, do you want evidence that faith without deeds is useless? Was not our ancestor Abraham considered righteous for what he did when he offered his son Isaac on the altar? You see that his faith and his actions were working together, and his faith was made complete by what he did. And the scripture was fulfilled that says, "Abraham believed God, and it was credited to him as righteousness," and he was called God's friend. You see that a person is justified by what he does and not by faith alone.

In the same way, was not even Rahab the prostitute considered righteous for what she did when she gave lodging to the spies and sent them off in a different direction? As the body without the spirit is dead, so faith without deeds is dead.

YOUR OBSERVATION

Two people are mentioned in this passage: Abraham and Rahab. Using just the information provided here, what do you know about them?

YOUR REACTION

That last sentence is a powerful summary of the passage. Rewrite it in your own words, using an example from your own life. (Example: Like a car without gas is dead, so is my example for Jesus on the football field dead if I play selfishly.)

◣ YOUR DISCOVERY

The two examples of righteous people James refers to couldn't be more different. On one hand there is Abraham, known for being a man of faith who leaves behind everything to follow God into a new land. Through this action, God creates the nation of Israel out of his descendants.

On the other hand, some Jewish historians believe Rahab became a prostitute at ten years old and lived this life for forty years.[8] She isn't a Jew and doesn't know God personally, but she believes in his power from reputation alone. When some Israelite spies are going to be captured, Rahab takes a step of faith by helping them and affirming her faith in the Lord (Joshua 2:11).

In our language, it's like Abraham is a church kid and Rahab is unchurched but finds the way in through God's grace. Both of them are mentioned here to show us that anyone can take a real step of faith, if it's genuine and is backed up by action. However you'd grade your life between these two people, we all need to take another step toward Jesus, whether it's your first, fiftieth, or five thousandth.

◣ YOUR CHALLENGE

Your good deeds won't save you, but they might help save someone else.

It's true that Jesus died for you because nothing you do could ever fill in the huge gap that sin created between you and God. Isaiah 64:6 reminds us that even our best attempt at a good deed is like throwing a filthy, stained rag before the Lord that we pretend is clean. Since Christ is the one we turn to for our rescue, some people believe this means they don't need to do anything productive for God.

When you choose to be faithful, though, people get a chance to see Jesus in ways they otherwise would have missed out on. He said that we are like a light in this world, and we need to let that light shine before others so they can see the Father through our good deeds. That's why James even mentions Abraham and Rahab in this passage, so we can get inspired by their examples.

Think about the areas of your life where you are afraid to be who God made you to be. Maybe there's fear because you wonder if someone might make fun of you for believing in something you can't see with your eyes. It's ironic because, if you would live out your faith in courage, then they would have something to see with their eyes: a follower of Christ who is completely his.

If you were to join the military, you'd get new clothes, a fresh haircut, and be trained to ditch your old attitude. As you walked around town, people would recognize you for being a part of something greater than yourself. Your new life would be represented by these changes.

What's weird is that Christians seem to take the opposite approach. We're so spooked that someone will see we're different that we blend in and lose our identities in the process. Is that worth someone else missing out on God and heaven, just so you can be thought of as common?

Your good deeds won't save you, but they might help save someone else.

 YOUR APPLICATION

Fill in these two columns—what you say about your faith and what you do because of your faith:

What I Say about My Faith
Example: I say I have a new life.

What I Do Because of My Faith
Example: I stopped telling dirty jokes.

DAY 20

YOUR STARTING POINT

James 3:1-2

Not many of you should presume to be teachers, my brothers, because you know that we who teach will be judged more strictly. We all stumble in many ways. If anyone is never at fault in what he says, he is a perfect man, able to keep his whole body in check.

YOUR OBSERVATION

Why does James mention that someone shouldn't presume to be a teacher without first considering it?

YOUR REACTION

Who is someone in your life whom you think understood the responsibility of being a teacher to others? What stands out to you about this person?

YOUR DISCOVERY

The early church is spreading fast when James writes this, and a lot of people in Jerusalem look to him as their leader. Instead of building himself up, he again points out how everyone stumbles, including him. He doesn't want anyone thinking teachers are above being judged.

Compare that to our world today and how often people fight against being held accountable for their actions. Maybe you can think of someone famous who has made some bad choices or even someone you personally know. Think about whom that person's bad decisions have affected in one way or another.

None of this should discourage you from stepping forward to lead others in what you've learned about God, but it should encourage you to do so with the right attitude and actions. James and other Christian leaders step into a role of spiritual leadership that Jewish rabbis have gone to school for. He mentions that our words are a big area we need to pay special attention to, especially because we often mess up and lose our credibility with others. This is one reason it's important to establish your identity in the truths of the Bible. The more time you spend memorizing truth, the less likely you are to speak lies.

 ## YOUR CHALLENGE

Of the people in your life you look up to, think about why you give them authority over you. In some cases, maybe that person has an official title or position, such as a teacher or boss. It could be that you follow a person because that person is exciting to be around, like an older sibling or kid in your neighborhood. There are some people you are willing to listen to because they have something solid to say that speaks to your life, like a youth worker or pastor.

The Bible records how Jesus at times feels like the people around him are like sheep without a shepherd.[9] Much hasn't changed today; some of your friends or family are walking around lost too. What do you think it's going to take for them to bust out of this daze and actually follow Christ?

They're going to have to see him, and that's where you come in.

When you look back on your high school years, what will stand out about who you were? Will you think about the haircut you picked, changed to, or changed back to? What clothing will you laugh about that you actually wore, from your weird shoes to your odd pants? Will it matter what music you listened to or how many yearbook photos you showed up in?

Or might you think back on something larger? Will there be a defining moment when you decided that you were going to become a leader by following Jesus and showing others how to do the same?

That moment can start right now.

YOUR APPLICATION

Devote yourself to the service of Jesus Christ. Write a letter of devotion to him right here, as if you are pledging yourself for the rest of your life. Consider what this means for you one year, three years, five years, seven years, and ten years from now.

DAY 21

ID CHECK

Read: Colossians 1:13-14

What have you learned in the past six days about who God says you can become?

In what areas might you be falling short the most in claiming your God-given identity?

What is one action step you can put into place over the next seven days to grow more fully into your identity in Christ?

DAY 22

James 3:3-8

When we put bits into the mouths of horses to make them obey us, we can turn the whole animal. Or take ships as an example. Although they are so large and are driven by strong winds, they are steered by a very small rudder wherever the pilot wants to go. Likewise the tongue is a small part of the body, but it makes great boasts. Consider what a great forest is set on fire by a small spark. The tongue also is a fire, a world of evil among the parts of the body. It corrupts the whole person, sets the whole course of his life on fire, and is itself set on fire by hell. All kinds of animals, birds, reptiles and creatures of the sea are being tamed and have been tamed by man, but no man can tame the tongue. It is a restless evil, full of deadly poison.

◂ YOUR OBSERVATION

If no human being can tame the tongue, then who is the only one who can?

▮ YOUR REACTION

Think over the past week, and write down at least one example of how something could have gone better if you or another person had a tamed tongue versus a loose one.

◤ YOUR DISCOVERY

When James uses the word *hell*, there are two ways to understand it. There's the reality of hell as a place of future punishment, and there is also a place known in the first century as Gehenna. This is a sewer channel where people in Jerusalem toss their garbage, human waste, and dead animals so it can all be burned. So not only is James pointing out that a loose tongue can be used by Satan in harmful ways but that it's full of rank garbage that can pollute the very air we breathe.

YOUR CHALLENGE

Have you ever played around with a boomerang? It takes some skill to throw it properly, but a boomerang is shaped to come back to you. God created the laws of physics and aerodynamics in such a way that when you intentionally throw a boomerang out in the right way, it can return to you.

There is also a way to throw a boomerang that's a wasted throw. If you don't handle it in the right way or throw it at the right angle, it will simply fall to the ground—or worse, injure someone or damage something. This isn't what a boomerang was designed to do, but if you don't follow the instructions, you will waste its potential.

Our words are the same way, and they have a purpose not only to soar but to come back to us in a positive way. If we are reckless with them, however, they will fall to the ground—or worse, injure someone. We'll waste so many opportunities if we don't follow the instructions (the Bible) that God has given us to use them in a way that brings life and joy around us.

Jesus Christ is the ultimate example of this for us, throwing out his life on the cross in order to return life to us. What he said on earth made such an impact that we're still talking about it two thousand years later. Which raises the question: Is what comes out of your mouth so genuine and Christ centered that people will even be talking about it a week from now? This won't happen if you try to say something important; it will happen by becoming someone who actually has something important to say.

▶ YOUR APPLICATION

Rate yourself in each of these areas:

(O) I often do this

(S) I sometimes do this

(R) I rarely do this.

____ I exaggerate things so I can look good

____ I don't tell the whole story when I want to protect myself from getting in trouble

____ I swear a lot

____ I rip others to shreds with my words when I'm around certain people

____ I say what I think, even if it hurts

____ I cut people off or interrupt them so I can speak

____ I constantly tell people what they need to do better, even if they didn't ask

____ I flatter people to get them to give me what I want.

____ I don't speak up, even if it would help another person

DAY 23

YOUR STARTING POINT

YOUR STARTING POINT

James 3:9-12

With the tongue we praise our Lord and Father, and with it we curse men, who have been made in God's likeness. Out of the same mouth come praise and cursing. My brothers, this should not be. Can both fresh water and salt water flow from the same spring? My brothers, can a fig tree bear olives, or a grapevine bear figs? Neither can a salt spring produce fresh water.

YOUR OBSERVATION

Why might cursing another person be horrible enough that it's mentioned in these verses?

YOUR REACTION

Read these verses again. How do you need to grow in this area?

YOUR DISCOVERY

It is a common habit for Jews to respond to the mention of God's name with the phrase "Blessed is he!"[10] In addition to the other prayers and praises offered each day, it is obviously hypocritical to then turn around and curse at other people. Sometimes that happens when you regularly take part in a spiritual community. You begin to do things mechanically that don't impact the other areas of your life.

To paint a picture of how foolish this is and how God wants to transform us, James uses the example of fresh water and salt water flowing from the same spring. This may trigger a memory among the Jews and early Christians of how Moses once threw a piece of wood into a certain body of water, changing it from bitter to sweet.[11] Although at the time it was simply a way to offer fresh water for people who were thirsty, it also contains symbolism of what Jesus has done for us on the cross. By casting himself down in the bitter waters of our hearts, he can transform every area of our lives (including our speech) into something sweet and refreshing. That may be a reason James uses this metaphor here—to show that we have to pick one or the other. But if we choose the way of Jesus, all things are possible, including language that adds to our world.

YOUR CHALLENGE

Picture this scene that you're probably familiar with: A group of teenagers is sitting around, and their energy plays off each other. Someone makes a quick remark about another person who isn't there, and then everyone chimes in and rips that person to shreds. Maybe they're talking about how easy a girl or guy is or how someone else is a freak that nobody likes.

Now, *where* is this conversation taking place?

Think about that for a moment. Do you imagine this happening in a fast-food restaurant while everyone blows off some steam after school? Is it all taking place in a school cafeteria, locker room, or in the bleachers of a sporting event? Is the conversation taking place on a road trip, or while everyone hangs out at someone's house?

Or might this all be taking place in a church environment? Does a prayer request time suddenly turn into a gossip session? Is a group of student leaders ripping on other youth who don't come to church anymore—only, instead of their hearts breaking, they become judgmental? Might a pastor or youth leader ask for an example of a bad choice, and, rather than everyone examining their own lives, they choose to criticize others?

What's scary is that any of these examples could be true. While we need to remember that those who don't know Jesus might be doing this out in the world, the warning from these Bible verses is that there is simply no place for it in the life of a Christian or the church. That's not going to happen if we simply try not to talk bad about people but only if we let God break us on this from the inside. Part of your renewed identity in Jesus means seeing people as he sees them so that your speech can breathe life instead of condemn others to death.

 YOUR APPLICATION

Different circumstances or people set us off in unique ways. Circle the responses that best describe how you react in each situation:

When I get made fun of by others my age . . .

I make fun of someone else to feel better

I shut down and get all moody

I laugh it off

I think of a way to put them down even more

I put my head down

I pray for the people who made fun of me

I tell an adult

I start swearing

I write horrible things about them

When my family gets on my nerves . . .

I talk with them personally about it

I tease siblings until they get frustrated

I whine until someone notices me

I yell at someone

I pull away

I pray for whoever started it

I talk with an adult

I write horrible things about them

I start swearing

DAY 24

YOUR STARTING POINT

James 3:13-18

Who is wise and understanding among you? Let him show it by his good life, by deeds done in the humility that comes from wisdom. But if you harbor bitter envy and selfish ambition in your hearts, do not boast about it or deny the truth. Such "wisdom" does not come down from heaven but is earthly, unspiritual, of the devil. For where you have envy and selfish ambition, there you find disorder and every evil practice. But the wisdom that comes from heaven is first of all pure; then peace-loving, considerate, submissive, full of mercy and good fruit, impartial and sincere. Peacemakers who sow in peace raise a harvest of righteousness.

YOUR OBSERVATION

What are the two things this passage notes are the evidence of false wisdom?

YOUR REACTION

The true wisdom from heaven is painted as pure, peace-loving, considerate, submissive, full of mercy and good fruit, impartial, and sincere. Whom do you personally know who seems to have this kind of character?

YOUR DISCOVERY

Basically, there are two weird truths we need to understand as we make choices on what to do and how to do it. The wisdom of the world, such as the things others tell you so you can get what you want, may seem to make sense and even appear as if it works for a while. However, it produces confusion, heartache, and things that distract us from God. In contrast, the wisdom of God may not always give the impression that it makes sense and will work, but it creates a peace beyond understanding, unity among Christians, and hope in this world.

James does his best to live this out personally and help others in the early church adopt this practice. As the initial spread of Christianity grows, several different issues come up that everyone seems to have a passionate opinion about. One of them is whether Gentiles (people who aren't Jews) need to take part in some of the practices and behaviors of the Jews. James plays a big role in one of these discussions, saying, "It is my judgment, therefore, that we should not make it difficult for the Gentiles who are turning to God."[12] He then suggests some ideas on how to help them lead a God-honoring life, which in turn becomes something other churches adopt.

Keep in mind, this wisdom may not be popular among even some of the early Christians, who may prefer feeling special. Sometimes even in churches, we struggle with making it easy for others to come to Jesus, while in other congregations things become too watered down. There is a reason that, even in the midst of controversy, James's words are accepted. It brings more people to Jesus without compromising the holiness of God.

YOUR CHALLENGE

It's tempting to live life amazed at our own brilliance. Of course, that's a sarcastic comment, but it's still true. We can become so "smart" about life that we never let anyone speak truth and hard love into us. Our first response to people who try to offer us something to think about is, "I know!" or, "I tried that already!" Rather than ask new questions that might reverse old conclusions, we can begin to live in the comfortable idea and selfish ambition that we can't possibly be wrong.

There are other times, though, that we live in a place of envy. As this passage puts it, we disguise it with wise words so we don't give it away. Still, we say things like, "Shawn would probably do well at playing football with us. But you know, we'll have to hold his hand because he doesn't know the plays like we do." Or, "Tina has a pretty voice, although I am glad we can't hear how loud it is when we're in choir." Sometimes we push people off a cliff with our words and quickly cover our tracks because we're threatened by someone else's popularity or skills, like some secret game of King of the Hill.

Having a God-centered idea means we choose to celebrate others, even when we'd like to steal the spotlight. That's actually the best way to deal with jealousy and self-centeredness—to praise God for how he created another person and the unique gifts that person brings into the world. That way we keep coming back to his identity in order to better form our own identities in him and not in our accomplishments.

YOUR APPLICATION

What comes out of our mouths can build countries and start wars; can cause one man to drop his gun and another to fire his; can make a mere house a loving home or a loving home a mere house; can make people see what they were blind to or people blind to what they no longer can see.

Out of the overflow of our hearts, our mouths will speak. This means the wisdom you live by will determine the way you impact others. All of this tracks back to where we base our identities and whether we have teachable spirits or arrogant notions that we're much wiser and more mature than others.

Since it's virtually impossible to check our own hearts, think about what has come out of your mouth lately:

T: Truth

> My speech is more full of: Opinions, or truth?

H: Helpful

> My conversations tend to: Make life harder for others, or help others?

I: Inspired

> My everyday speech is more: "Look at me," or "Look at God"?

N: Necessary

> My ideas are typically: Just so I can talk, or necessary ideas that add to the lives of others?

K: Kind

> My tone is usually: Critical, or harmful?

DAY 25

James 4:1-3

What causes fights and quarrels among you? Don't they come from your desires that battle within you? You want something but don't get it. You kill and covet, but you cannot have what you want. You quarrel and fight. You do not have, because you do not ask God. When you ask, you do not receive, because you ask with wrong motives, that you may spend what you get on your pleasures.

YOUR OBSERVATION

Jesus teaches in the Lord's Prayer the attitude of "not my will, but yours be done." How would that type of thinking help the people James seems to be talking to here?

YOUR REACTION

Be honest. Do you seek God for a relationship with him (i.e., "God, whether or not you give me what I want, I love you. Thanks for being the core of my life!"), or for what having a relationship with him offers you (i.e., "I always like how praising God through songs makes me feel!")?

▲ YOUR DISCOVERY

The first Christians live in a culture marked by Hellenization. That's a big word that describes how the Greeks are trying to spread their culture, language, and beliefs to everything. Although some of their ideas are outright rejected, other ideas that are more appealing begin to shape some of the ways the early church lives. The book of Revelation starts out with seven letters to seven churches that get more into this, but James is trying to get to the root of this issue by warning against the pursuit of pleasure.

Again, this may seem like a no-brainer that we would catch and be on our guard against. Even in our culture today, though, there can be a sense that God wants us to be happy. He doesn't, by the way. God wants you to be *holy*. So much of what Jesus teaches deals with denying our urges and asking, *Who is God? Who am I because of who God is? And what choice makes the most sense to honor all of that?*

James has been called many things by historians and scholars, but the thing they all seem to agree on is that he is incredibly practical. As he points out in these verses, we're likely to settle for anything that sounds good to calm our urges when we feel empty or frustrated. This leads to problems with others who either want the same things or try to point out what we might be blind to.

YOUR CHALLENGE

Loneliness and feeling disconnected are temptations we will all deal with. You can go to a school of 1,500 people and feel alone; you can take part in a church or youth group and feel alone; you can go home and feel alone. Sometimes we handle this well, and other times we go looking for something to fill us up or make us feel something.

It can get really bad sometimes too. If you've ever seen a well-trained dog or cat turn on its master when the animal isn't feeling fed, you know how something that once was gentle can become irritable and dangerous to others. You may even see them eat things that aren't food at all, just so their bellies can feel like something is in them.

Our spiritual, emotional, physical, and intellectual hungers can do the same thing. We may feel frustrated with God, so we add other religious belief system to our faith. We may be jealous of what other people have, so we get into arguments with them. We may want to feel loved, so we settle for sexual attention that fades as quickly as it arrives. We may want to look smart, so we do whatever we can to make others feel dumb.

Consider where you spend a lot of your time. If you're looking for a purpose in life but most of your week is full of video games, hanging out online, or getting one step cozier with someone you feel attracted to, you're likely trying to fill the belly of your life with something that looks like food but won't give you any real nourishment. If you aren't sure, ask yourself whom you are arguing with these days and why. Maybe it's your parents who want something better for you, or maybe it's God himself. You can learn a lot from an argument, including what urges seem to be driving your side of it.

 YOUR APPLICATION

Read Psalm 1, and rewrite it in your own words according to your own temptations and victories in life these days.

DAY 26

YOUR STARTING POINT

James 4:4-10

You adulterous people, don't you know that friend-ship with the world is hatred toward God? Anyone who chooses to be a friend of the world becomes an enemy of God. Or do you think Scripture says without reason that the spirit he caused to live in us envies intensely? But he gives us more grace. That is why Scripture says: "God opposes the proud but gives grace to the humble." Submit yourselves, then, to God. Resist the devil, and he will flee from you. Come near to God and he will come near to you. Wash your hands, you sinners, and purify your hearts, you double-minded. Grieve, mourn and wail. Change your laughter to mourning and your joy to gloom. Humble yourselves before the Lord, and he will lift you up.

YOUR OBSERVATION

Why do you think God opposes the proud but gives grace to the humble? What do you think this means?

YOUR REACTION

We're told to specifically resist the devil in order to make him flee from us. How often when you're tempted do you specifically and consciously do this, versus just trying to not give into temptation?

YOUR DISCOVERY

In this passage, James talks about the "spirit who lives in us" as one who "envies intensely." Jealousy is usually a negative thing, and the Bible certainly uses it in this way. James seems to be tapping into something positive, though, that refers back to when the Lord gave Moses the Ten Commandments. He said, "Do not worship any other god, for the Lord, whose name is Jealous, is a jealous God."[13]

If you misunderstand this part of God's identity, he really sounds like an emotional whiner. Do you picture him sulking in the corner because we gave something or someone else our attention, or might God be more secure than that? After all, he really doesn't need us to like him for him to be God.

This kind of envy is something positive. He is jealous for you and your best interests. It's like parents who let their kids go off to college and know that they'll make some independent choices that may or may not be positive. The love those parents have includes a wish list. They want their children to make the best decisions possible and will jealously speak against anyone or anything that might hurt their sons or daughters.

Envy like this isn't self-centered but is about the bigger picture. Instead of grouchiness, there is tenderness, for God watches over us and tries to steer us clear of things we keep drifting into. The Lord loves you so passionately that he can't bear a rival love that could destroy us.

YOUR CHALLENGE

Christians can give Jesus Christ a bad name, especially when people who talk about following Jesus live in such a way that they try to get whatever they want. It's a primary reason we're challenged not to be friends with the world but to live in it without becoming like it. Otherwise we confuse everyone around us who is watching, which many people are. Even when people genuinely give their lives to Jesus, it is easier for them to take their cues from what other Christians are and are not doing than it is to understand God's priorities and desires for their own lives.

Think about a time when you let a friend come hang out with you and your extended family. Maybe there's an oddly outspoken uncle or aunt whom you have to keep apologizing for, or a cousin or sibling who is nothing like you or your friend. God doesn't want us to feel this way about each other, which is why he challenges us to stay humble and keep growing. People are looking for a reason to reject Christ, but if they were honest, they are actually looking for someone who is the real deal.

Are you all talk and no show? Sometimes people can be unfair about this, maybe because they were hurt by Christians, so they watch you with ten magnifying glasses, hoping you mess up so they can feel justified. This is all the more reason not to fake a good life but to live an authentic one. By walking the walk you talk, maybe you can actually begin to redefine Christianity in someone else's mind.

Or, you can keep doing what everyone else your age is doing. Go to the next school dance and grind up against someone, or party on the weekend and show up to a church service out of obligation. Get caught up in hours upon hours of movies and media, and post every picture online for others to compliment your lifestyle.

Then again, maybe you can recognize that there is something more important than that. Sure, you'll make mistakes that others will notice. So use that, saying, "Thank you for noticing that. I'm a work in progress, and I need people around me to help me catch stuff I'm missing. Since you caught that, would you help me grow in that area?"

YOUR APPLICATION

The promise in this passage is, "Come near to God, and he will come near to you." Make a list of 8-10 things you will do in the next week to draw near to God on purpose.

DAY 27

⬈ YOUR STARTING POINT

James 4:11-12

Brothers and sisters, do not slander one another. Anyone who speaks against a brother or sister or judges them speaks against the law and judges it. When you judge the law, you are not keeping it, but sitting in judgment on it. There is only one Lawgiver and Judge, the one who is able to save and destroy. But you—who are you to judge your neighbor?

◣ YOUR OBSERVATION

Obviously, Christians should get along and speak life into one another. Yet these verses are here on purpose, so maybe it's not always so obvious to us. What reasons do you think fellow Christians might slander each other?

▮ YOUR REACTION

How have you seen the idea of not judging your neighbor be misused by people who want to do what they want to do?

◤ YOUR DISCOVERY

James wisely warns us against putting each other down, pointing out that it's less of a reflection on them and more an insight about what's going on between us and God. This doesn't mean we shouldn't speak into one another's lives in directional ways but merely that we don't slander each other in the process. It's one thing to say, "Chris, I'm sensing that you're struggling with something you may not want me to talk to you about. Can I share it with you?" It's another thing entirely to say, "Chris, you really blew it. You're such a loser. I can't figure out why we were ever friends." One approach brings a person to God for growth, while the other uses God's standards as a weapon.

This is a fine line that even the early church struggles with. Through the thousands of Pharisees (religious experts) living at the time, there is a sense in the old Jewish way of thinking that we should measure each other based on how we live. If a person doesn't follow the rules in the Hebrew Scriptures as well as those the Pharisees have come up with, everyone else is encouraged to label that person and separate themselves from that person.

Jesus said, though, that he came to seek and save the lost.[14] Notice that he does call people "lost," but it isn't to slander them or judge them. It is to recognize them and offer them hope in him. We're called to join in that example.

 ## YOUR CHALLENGE

There's an old saying that goes, "If you can't say something nice, don't say anything at all." That's a nice sentiment, but it is incomplete. Part of being the church to one another isn't just speaking things that sound good but *are* good. Often we bottle up our thoughts, which end up feeding a critical spirit we use to look at and judge everyone else.

Most of the time we don't even see the seriousness of this until it impacts another person or our own sense of peace. We start to sense that something isn't quite right with our lives, but instead of getting the perspective from others that we need, it becomes easy to think they're the problem. All of a sudden, we're trying to win debates or look better than fellow Christians rather than speaking kindly to one another.

Imagine that you own a highly intelligent parrot that can repeat the things you say about other people. Would you be comfortable selling that parrot, or would you be afraid of what it would repeat? Maybe that's why the verses before this talk about washing *your* hands—the hands of the person who enjoys criticizing.

 YOUR APPLICATION

Make ten cards that have the following words written on them: *I don't need to win this argument because my relationship with the person giving me this card is more important.* Give them to the people in your life whom you find yourself debating or criticizing often, and tell those people to give the cards to you when you start getting critical so you can remember there is something greater at play than you proving them wrong.

DAY 28

ID CHECK

Read: 2 Corinthians 1:21-22

What have you learned in the past six days about who God says you can become?

In what areas might you be falling short the most in claiming your God-given identity?

What is one action step you can put into place over the next seven days to grow more fully into your identity in Christ?

DAY 29

James 4:13-17

Now listen, you who say, "Today or tomorrow we will go to this or that city, spend a year there, carry on business and make money." Why, you do not even know what will happen tomorrow. What is your life? You are a mist that appears for a little while and then vanishes. Instead, you ought to say, "If it is the Lord's will, we will live and do this or that." As it is, you boast and brag. All such boasting is evil. Anyone, then, who knows the good he ought to do and doesn't do it, sins.

YOUR OBSERVATION

Our lives are compared to a mist in this passage. What other metaphors would you use to describe how short life actually is in the grand scheme of eternity?

YOUR REACTION

If you had to choose one or the other, would you rather be able to plan out your life or not know what's coming next? Why?

YOUR DISCOVERY

Different pieces of the Bible can seem to be oddly arranged sometimes. For example, in this passage James talks about the dangers of planning your life, only to end his thought with a challenge against sinning. Specifically, he says that if you don't do what you know you're supposed to do, it's as bad as if you violated a specific command from the Bible.

This isn't quite as disconnected as you may think. The early church lives during a dangerous time when people barely have enough money to get by and constantly live in fear of being persecuted for their faith. It's easy during such moments for people to brainstorm ways out of their trouble because hardship isn't easy and can choke the life out of us if we let it.

Perhaps this is why James juxtaposes the two seemingly different topics—because, often when we know that God wants us to endure something hard, we'd rather come up with ways to soften the blow than forge ahead in courage. By reminding Christians of this through these words, the Lord uses James to ask us which is more important—to be in control of our lives, or to pick up our crosses and follow Christ. The upside of giving things to God is that, while you don't know what your future holds, you know who holds your future.

 YOUR CHALLENGE

All right, time to pony up. What has God asked you to do that you'd rather not do?

Has he challenged you to share what you've found in him with another person or a group of people? Is there a habit he's nudged you to take up or let go of? Have you sensed him leading you to change something in your life that you currently find comfort in? Even if you just look at the Bible alone, there are plenty of challenges like this that we seem to ignore.

Or we can find humor in the things that break God's heart; we can seek thrills over spring break just because everyone else is. Or we can talk about how we're able to handle things we shouldn't be handling in the first place.

This isn't being brought up to send you on a guilt trip. Rather, you are reading these very words right now because it's time to call it out for what it is. Namely, God has asked you to do something, and to not do it is sinning.

So, what are you going to do with that?

 YOUR APPLICATION

Write down five things that, if God asked you to give them up, you'd argue with him over.

Write down three things the Lord has asked you to do but that you haven't yet done.

Read Ephesians 6:18 and 1 John 5:14-15. Write down any final observations that any of this stirs up for you.

DAY 30

James 5:1-6

Now listen, you rich people, weep and wail because of the misery that is coming upon you. Your wealth has rotted, and moths have eaten your clothes. Your gold and silver are corroded. Their corrosion will testify against you and eat your flesh like fire. You have hoarded wealth in the last days. Look! The wages you failed to pay the workmen who mowed your fields are crying out against you. The cries of the harvesters have reached the ears of the Lord Almighty. You have lived on earth in luxury and self-indulgence. You have fattened yourselves in the day of slaughter. You have condemned and murdered innocent men, who were not opposing you.

◀ YOUR OBSERVATION

The rich are called out for the way they have treated the poor. What do you think the responsibility is of people who have a lot of money when it comes to how they talk with or deal with people who are really hurting financially?

◼ YOUR REACTION

What is some of the stuff in your life that you really enjoy owning and having?

YOUR DISCOVERY

Oddly enough, James talks about gold and silver corroding away like rust. Most people in his era know this isn't the way it works. These metals don't rust but seem to stand the test of time. It is as if he is saying that even what seems indestructible in our world will lose its value in God's kingdom. Or, as any civilization that has faced a natural disaster has learned, you can't buy your way out of death with any amount of money.

It's likely that this letter doesn't initially land on the ears of many rich people, for most of the first Christians are people who are poor and depend on their community supporting one another's needs. It might be easy to envy the rich, though, which is why James specifically tries to remove the desire to have stuff that will ultimately fade away and affect the quality of our relationships on earth.

Does this mean that being rich is wrong? Not at all, except that it shouldn't be our goal to become rich. A clearer perspective is to say, "God, however you bless me financially in life, it's all yours, and I will be as faithful in caring for others and supporting your church with one dollar as I would with a million dollars."

 ## YOUR CHALLENGE

Most people have an idea of a dream job. Often we'll work hard to get those dream jobs by showing up to one interview after another with our hair combed, our outfits ironed, and *go-get-em* attitudes.

The problem for many of us begins once we get the job. Now, instead of showing up on time with everything done, we may clock in and then go to the bathroom to fix our hair. Perhaps we'll stretch our break a few minutes extra, or when it's time to leave, we may shut down our effort at work five minutes before the official time and stand by the time clock with our coats on. Maybe you even begin to take advantage of the company's resources, by taking pens or paper home that someone there paid for.

We may not all be incredibly wealthy, but every one of us will encounter a situation like this. We will be in charge over the wealth of our opportunities, and we have to ask if we will let our identity in Christ guide us or if we'll take advantage of the system. The integrity you have in these moments can be louder than anything you might ever say to your coworkers, or it just might provide the opportunity to do so.

 YOUR APPLICATION

Spontaneously give away some money this week. Try something easy, something a little harder, and something really difficult. Use it as a way to remind yourself and declare to God that money isn't as important as we make it out to be.

DAY 31

YOUR STARTING POINT

James 5:7-20

Be patient, then, brothers, until the Lord's coming. See how the farmer waits for the land to yield its valuable crop and how patient he is for the autumn and spring rains. You too, be patient and stand firm, because the Lord's coming is near. Don't grumble against each other, brothers, or you will be judged. The Judge is standing at the door! Brothers, as an example of patience in the face of suffering, take the prophets who spoke in the name of the Lord. As you know, we consider blessed those who have persevered. You have heard of Job's perseverance and have seen what the Lord finally brought about. The Lord is full of compassion and mercy.

Above all, my brothers, do not swear—not by heaven or by earth or by anything else. Let your "Yes" be yes, and your "No," no, or you will be condemned. Is any one of you in trouble? He should pray. Is anyone happy? Let him sing songs of praise. Is any one of you sick? He should call the elders of the church to pray over him and anoint him with oil in the name of the Lord. And the prayer offered in faith will make the sick person well; the Lord will raise him up. If he has sinned, he will be forgiven. Therefore confess your sins to each other and pray for each other so that you may be healed. The prayer of a righteous man is powerful and effective. Elijah was a man just like us. He prayed earnestly that it would not rain, and it did not rain on the land for three and a half years. Again he prayed, and the heavens gave rain, and the earth produced its crops. My brothers, if one of you should wander from the truth and someone should bring him back, remember this: Whoever turns a sinner from the error of his way will save him from death and cover over a multitude of sins.

YOUR OBSERVATION

You just read a big chunk of Scripture. Circle the ideas that most stand out to you.

 YOUR REACTION

When life gets tough, do you most tend to put the focus on how hard things are for you, or do you rally others to something greater—perhaps God himself? Why?

YOUR DISCOVERY

In everything James has covered throughout this whole book, he lands on two themes—suffering and sinners. Most letters like this typically end with a blessing or signature greeting, but James opts for a typical Greek format—to close with a purpose statement. In this case, he chooses to remind his readers that everything God has inspired him to write is for the purpose of reaching other people with the good news.

All the time spent on suffering just before that, though, reminds us how easy it is to think about life in our own little slice of it. When we become so consumed by this that we take our eyes off God, there is hope that we can be brought back to our true identities in him. In fact, walking through our suffering with the Lord instead of putting on a fake smile is one of the ways we learn more about him and ourselves that we would have otherwise missed out on.

YOUR CHALLENGE

Some days it feels like today is the day everything is going to fall apart. All the stress and trials and hardships that come along can be rough and cause us to only see the problems in front of us.

Life can mess you up sometimes. It can make you nearsighted. We say things like:

My family is a mess.
School takes everything out of me.
An old relationship keeps causing problems for me.
My parents don't listen.
I can't manage everyone else and all of their desires for my life.

You ever have a season like that? Sometimes all we can see in this life is our own problems. We forget that there is more going on than what just happened.

Our God is good, great, and powerful and knows what you're going through. He's able to meet that need, and he is right there with you.

His name is I AM.

Just look at the vastness of his creation. When your problems get too big to take, just consider how intricate and intelligent everything is. How certain bugs exist to eat other bugs, which exist to eat certain things that keep us healthy. Or how our bodies are able to take what we eat and turn the good parts into human tissue and get rid of the bad parts. Or how life can appear when science says it can't, doctors say there is no hope, and hope says all is lost. Or how the position of the earth and moon and sun are so precise that even the slightest percentage of difference would cause crazy ripples, and yet somehow they are held together.

And right now, as you consider all of this and decide whether you want to receive it or debate it, you have a complex brain that works in ways you can't even fathom. Where did that brain come from? Who created it so unique and complex?

His name is I AM.

He knows every star and every planet and every constellation, and he knows you by name. Can you imagine? In comparison to the size of this universe we know, we are less than insignificant. We are seen and known and understood and loved. Loved by him.

His name is I AM.

We are not even as bright as the sun or as large as a galaxy, and yet the great God of the universe knows us, cares for us, loves us.

Do you get that?

So why do we doubt? Why do we fear? Why don't we trust that God can provide for us as he always has for his people? Why do we take our eyes off the big picture of loving God and helping others know how to have a relationship with him?

A poet named Helen Mallicoat described it in her own words this way:

I was regretting the past and fearing the future.
Suddenly, my Lord was speaking. He paused. I waited. He continued:

"When you live in the past, with its mistakes and regrets, it is hard.
I am not there. My name is not—I WAS.
When you live in the future, with its problems and fears, it is hard.
I am not there. My name is not—I WILL BE.

When you live in this moment, it is not hard.
I am here.
My name is I AM.[15]

Whatever happens, he's got our backs because he has our now. When you allow your identity to be anchored to him, you can use the struggles in life to look for God in ways that the joys distract us from.

His name is I AM.

YOUR APPLICATION

Tell a Christian and non-Christian friend why you love God and what you're learning about him. Write down a description of their responses here.

AFTERWORD

Life as you know it has just begun.

You have been given a gift over the past 31 days (or however long it took you to read this) of some hard-hitting questions. You may still struggle in certain areas. That's because you aren't perfect. But because you have taken this journey, you now can move forward without being a phony either.

With God all things are possible, so you may find yourself immediately feeling free from old stuff. Or, you may still have to endure some of the circumstances you initially walked into this with. Either way, remember that your goal isn't to look more Christian but simply to follow Jesus and let the rest take care of itself.

So what's next?

That's a big question that you need to take before God. Maybe you need to go back and reread this book with a friend, or maybe you need to do another walk through a different book of the Bible and let what you read speak life into you.

One thing is for sure, though: We will be transformed by the renewing of our minds. So get your brain in gear around some great truths. The world won't stop trying to tell you who you are.

But perhaps you now know that its screams aren't as powerful as the whispers of God. He doesn't have the same expectations on you that a lot of other people in your life do.

God doesn't require you to be cool to be accepted.
God doesn't avoid you if you aren't wearing name-brand labels.
God isn't asking you to be just like someone else at school or in your family.

God hasn't turned away from you based on how your body does or doesn't look, how your grades score or don't score, or how active your social life is or isn't.

As you close this book, enjoy the amazing truth of that. Let it put a big smile on your face because the God of the universe knows your name, and he has told you who you really are.

NOTES

1. Mark 6:3 suggests James to be one of the blood siblings of Jesus, although some historians interpret this differently.

2. Josephus's *Antiquities*. Book 20, chapter 9.

3. Eusebius's *Ecclesiastical History*. Vol. II, chapter 23 (A.D. 323).

4. *http://www.jewishencyclopedia.com/view.jsp?artid=142&letter=N.*

5. Job 2:10.

6. Genesis 3:12.

7. Jewish New Testament Commentary by Daniel Stern, pp 730-731.

8. http://www.jewishencyclopedia.com/view.jsp?letter=R&artid=71.

9. Mark 6:34, Matthew 9:36.

10. The Letters of James and Peter, William Barclay, p. 105.

11. Exodus 15:25.

12. Acts 15:19.

13. Exodus 34:14.

14. Luke 19:10

15. Helen Mallicoat. "I Am." Poster for Argus Communications. 1982.

To my Lord, my bride, my kids, and my church—
all of whom put Life into my life.